stionnaire du Vin Le Questionn

Sauvignon bla   i

Wine Questionnaire

Riesling Ch

CHÂTEAU
BORDEAUX
MARGAUX

re Le Questionnaire du Vi

e Wine Questionnaire pinot

Questionnaire Le Questionna

blanc Bordeaux

e Questionnaire Wine

Vin Chardonnay

rlot The Wine Questionna

Riesling pinot Wine

D1524827

The Wine Questionnaire

© 2012 Assouline Publishing
601 West 26th Street, 18th Floor
New York, NY 10001 USA
Tel.: 212-989-6810 Fax: 212-647-0005
www.assouline.com

ISBN: 978 1 61428 051 4

Illustrations by Samantha Hahn.
Pages 10-11: © Laziz Hamani
Page 57: © Paul Reid/Shutterstock.com
Printed in Canada.

Introduction by Jay McInerney

The Wine Questionnaire

ASSOULINE

Introduction
by Jay McInerney

I'm sorry to say that Marcel Proust had no hand in the creation of the questionnaire named after him. In fact, the authorship of the questionnaire is a mystery. Proust first encountered a version of it at the birthday party of his friend Antoinette Faure (daughter of the future French president) when he was thirteen. It was part of a confession album that was popular among English families at the time; the questions in Antoinette's album were in English, although young Proust answered them in French. In answer to the first question, "What do You Regard as the Lowest Depth of Misery?" the once and future Mama's boy responded, "To be Separated from Mama." Seven years later, at another social event, Proust filled out an almost identical questionnaire. The answers of the twenty-year-old Proust are more mature and erudite, although he still regards his mother as the center of his life. (To the question, "What to Your Mind would be the greatest of misfortunes?" he answers, "Not to have known my mother and grandmother.") The quality that he most admired in a man was "feminine charm," while the quality he most liked in a woman was "a man's virtues." Unfortunately, none of the questions address the subject of wine, and recently I was asked to redress this omission by creating a Proustian wine questionnaire. Judging by *À la recherche du temps perdu,* the great man himself seems to have been more interested in sweets than in fermented grape juice—at least, such was the case with his younger alter ego.

Brillat-Savarin famously remarked, "Tell me what you eat and I'll tell you what you are." To which we retort, "Tell me what you drink and I will tell you who you are." Like the original questionnaire, our vinous version is designed to elucidate the character of the respondent. You can learn a lot about character and taste by posing certain dichotomies: Plato or Aristotle? Tolstoy or Dostoyevsky? Fitzgerald or Hemingway? Beatles or Stones? The archetypal great divide in the world of wine is between Bordeaux and Burgundy. (Faced with an enthusiast whose drinking was confined within the New World, we would rephrase the choice as "Cab or pinot?" even as we would try to mask our pity.) Just to begin at the beginning, pinot noir is hard to grow and wildly sensitive to storage conditions; cabernet easier on both counts. Bordeaux is certainly more reliable, and it is probably a more cerebral wine than Burgundy. If you know your vintages and your châteaux, you will get what you pay for in Bordeaux (though increasingly you will pay through the nose). Bordeaux is intellectual, but congenial. It shows up on time and it puts out. Burgundy is a wine that speaks more to the heart than to the head, and while it sometimes speaks in the most seductive tones, it can also be shrill and nasty. One night you're in heaven; the next night you get slapped in the face. Burgundy is like the girl with the curl: "When she was good, she was very, very good, and when she was bad, she was horrid."

Your Burgundy lover is apt to be more of a romantic, more of a risk taker, the Bordeaux man or woman more grounded and more level-headed. Julian Barnes, the novelist, who is one of the most sensible and cerebral people I know, loves Bordeaux, and thinks that Burgundy is absurd. I don't necessarily agree with him, but I would be surprised if he felt the opposite. Me, I'm the kind of guy who doesn't mind risking disappointment, heartbreak, and rejection in the pursuit of bliss, which is to say that I'm a Burgundy lover.

Of course, there are other regions where wine is made, and certain free-spirited oenophiles may favor one of these above either Burgundy or Bordeaux, which is why we ask for a favorite wine region. I've heard Robert Parker, aka the world's most powerful critic, say that if forced to choose one region it would be the Rhône, specifically the Southern Rhône. Parker is a big man with big appetites, and the wines of his beloved Châteauneuf-du-Pape are reliably voluptuous, and Rabelaisian in their generosity, although Rabelais himself seems to have preferred the wines of his native Loire. And if a respondent to the questionnaire picks the Loire as her favorite region, I can say with some assurance that she is a

6

true wine geek, possibly a sommelier; if a New Yorker, a resident of Brooklyn, her iPod loaded with new music by bands that I haven't yet heard—or heard of. Anyone who picks Italy's Piedmont region as their favorite has my vote as an original thinker and a connoisseur.

Thirty-five years after the famous Judgment of Paris, the contest organized by Steven Spurrier in which wines from the Napa Valley triumphed over top French growths in a blind tasting judged by French wine authorities, it behooves us to remember that Europe no longer has a monopoly on fine wine production. New World or Old World is one of the great divides of taste, and character. New World wines are almost inevitably bolder and more brash than their Old World counterparts, and they have their partisans. I know several great American entrepreneurs who believe that Napa cabernets are the ultimate expression of that grape. And I know of at least one English wine buff who prefers the big, rich chardonnays of Sonoma to their Burgundian counterparts. It's easy to propose that the back-slapping, G'day-mate, full-throttle character of South Australian shirazes is a reflection of the national character.

Choosing a favorite wine region isn't necessarily easy, given the fact that most of us like variety, but it's easier than choosing a single wine that we would drink for the rest of our lives if we could only choose one. This is a question to torment the thoughtful wine lover. I almost hate myself for proposing it; last night I woke up in the middle of the night still struggling with the questions after days of contemplation. Champagne is probably the most versatile of all wines, but do you really want to drink champagne with a grilled rib eye? Many Germans drink riesling with almost everything, including beef, but I'm not German. And yet lighter, high-acid white wines like riesling are in fact probably better suited to the way most of us eat now—our lighter, Mediterranean/Asian–inflected diet doesn't necessarily call out for claret. Yes, but... Do you really want to drink white wine for the rest of your life? I have several friends for whom the answer to this is an emphatic yes, like Greg Brewer, who makes exquisitely focused chardonnays in the Santa Rita Hills north of Santa Barbara. He'd choose Chablis in a heartbeat. For better or for worse, though, I can't quite get over the feeling that white wine is the equivalent of foreplay. Eventually I yearn for consummation. I envy those who have a quick, firm answer to this question, which drives me to equivocation, torn as I am between rosé champagne and a lighter red like Volnay.

Slightly easier than choosing one beverage for the rest of my life is choosing the best wine I ever had—in my case a 1955 La Mission-Haut-Brion, which I first encountered in 1995 when we were both exactly forty years old. I've had several bottles since, some almost as good, and I will never forget the taste of that wine, with its medley of tobacco, leather, spice, and earth notes, consumed under the gaze of a chubby Renoir maiden in an apartment on the Upper East Side of Manhattan.

Although the patron saint of the questionnaire does not seem to have been an oenophile, the episode of the madeleine is the archetype of a wine lover's experience. The scent and the taste of a certain wine can unleash a flood of involuntary memory, almost inevitably pleasant, since wine drinking tends to be celebratory. Having once drunk the 1961 Latour at a lunch in Highgate, many years ago, I was transported back to that afternoon, the company and the conversation, and even the smell of the wet earth in the English garden where we lunched, on the next occasion that I was lucky enough to have a glass of it.

Most wine lovers remember their first wine, for better or worse. Mine was a so-called pink Chablis from Almaden, vintage unknown, which I consumed on the lawn of Tanglewood with my first girlfriend, Joan Coughlin, while listening to The Who perform *Tommy*. I remember the sweetish, strawberry taste of the wine, just as the music and the taste of Joan's kiss and the smell of the cannabis wafting across the lawn from all sides—a bittersweet memory, since Joan is no longer with us. Drinking wine, it seems to me, is a way of bookmarking our memories. It's also a process of self-discovery, and if we are lucky it's one that we continue to pursue over many years. The answers to some of these questions may change over time, just as wine changes and develops in the bottle with the passing years.

Sofia Coppola
Screenwriter, film director, and producer

Your first wine memory.

MIXING RUBICON AND ORANGINA AS A KID.

Are you Burgundy or Bordeaux?

BURGUNDY.

New World or Old World?

CALIFORNIA.

Your favourite region. NAPA, I GREW UP THERE —SO, RUTHERFORD.

The best wine you ever tasted.

2005 RUBICON.

Your favourite food and wine pairing.

CASK OR RUBICON AND A PORTER HOUSE STEAK.

Your favourite winemaker or vineyard.

INGLENOOK.

The most valuable bottle you own.

'41 INGLENOOK.

The most undervalued bottle you own.

CHÂTEAU THUERRY ROSÉ.

What wine do you wish you could taste?

'71 J.J. PRUM TROCKENBEERENAUSLESE MOSEL - SAAR - RUWER WEHLENER SONNENUHR!

Your favourite partner in wine. MY HUSBAND, THOMAS.

Restaurant you frequent for its wine list. 21 HOUSE, OR IL BUCO OUT

What bottle of wine makes the best hostess gift? RUINART BRUT OR SOFIA BLANC DE BLANCS.

Every wine collection should include: A '71 KRUG BRUT.

Your favourite time to enjoy a glass. APERITIF.

Your favourite wine accessory. RABBIT WINE OPENER.

Your choice aperitif. ROSÉ IN THE SUMMER OR ICE COLD RUINART BRUT.

Your best adviser. MY DAD.

Your favourite champagne. RUINART AND KRUG.

If you could drink only one wine for the rest of your life, what would it be? PENNINO ZINFANDEL.

Your favourite wine quote or motto. JUST THE IDEA OF 'TERROIR' THAT'S TRUE ABOUT ANYTHING ARTISTIC.

Robert M. Parker, Jr.

Founder of The Wine Advocate;
contributing editor for Food & Wine *magazine and* Business Week

Your first wine memory. *1967 Domaine de la Solitude Châteauneuf-du-Pape.*

Are you Burgundy or Bordeaux? *As a hedonist, not a masochist—Bordeaux.*

New World or Old World? *Some new, but mostly old.*

Your favourite region. *Southern France—the Rhône and Bordeaux.*

The best wine you ever tasted. *1961 Latour à Pomerol—the authentic bottle.*

Your favourite food and wine pairing. *Daniel Boulud's braised short ribs with 1990 Rayas.*

What is your favourite exception to this rule: white with fish, red with meat?
Red wine with fish, especially tuna and salmon.

Your favourite winemaker or vineyard. *Vineyard—The sandy soils planted with old-vine grenache called Le Grand Pierre in Châteauneuf-du-Pape. Winemaker—Manfred Krankl.*

The most valuable bottle you own. *Was an 1803 Madeira, but I gave it to the former Commandant of the U.S. Marine Corps, General James T. Conway.*

The most undervalued bottle you own. *Any Châteauneuf-du-Pape.*

What wine do you wish you could taste? *A magnum or grand format of 1959 DRC La Tache.*

Your favourite partner in wine. *My wife, Patricia—she has a better palate.*

Restaurant you frequent for its wine list. *Veritas in New York City.*

What bottle of wine makes the best hostess gift? *First growth Bordeaux.*

Every wine collection should include: *A phony and/or bullshit detector.*

Your favourite time to enjoy a ~~glass~~ bottle. *A long and civilized lunch.*

Your favourite wine accessory. *A great corkscrew.*

Your choice aperitif. *Campari and soda.*

Your best adviser. *Wife Patricia.*

Your favourite book on wine. *1. A. J. Liebling's <u>Between Meals</u>, although technically not a wine book.*
2. <u>Oxford Companion to Wine</u>.

What country would you visit for its vineyards? *Italy.*

Your favourite champagne. *Brut Dom Pérignon*
Billecart-Salmon Brut Rosé
Blanc de blancs

If you could drink only one wine for the rest of your life, what would it be? *Red wines from the*
Rhône and Bordeaux.

Your favourite wine quote or motto. *"Always smell it first."*

BORDEAUX

André Balazs

Hotelier

Your first wine memory.

Rosé with my father at our home in St. Tropez.

Are you Burgundy or Bordeaux? *Burgundy!*

New World or Old World? *Old World!*

Your favourite region. *Côte de Nuits.*

The best wine you ever tasted. *Lafite-Rothschild 1996.*

Your favourite food and wine pairing. *Grilled Italian steak with Barbaresco.*

What is your favourite exception to this rule: white with fish, red with meat?

Chilled gamay with grilled fish.

Your favourite winemaker or vineyard. *Armand Rousseau, Gevrey-Chambertin.*

The most valuable bottle you own. *I prefer not to know.*

The most undervalued bottle you own. *'09 Village Burgundies, extraordinary value.*

What wine do you wish you could taste? *Romanée-Conti La Tache, 1880.*

Your favourite partner in wine. *A car and driver!*

Restaurant you frequent for its wine list. St. John, London.

What bottle of wine makes the best hostess gift? Domaine Ott.

Every wine collection should include: A case you shouldn't touch for at least 20 years.

Your favourite time to enjoy a glass. The last meeting of the day,

Your favourite wine accessory. Good company,

Your choice aperitif. Martini, stirred not shaken — Bond had it wrong,

Your best adviser. The wine directors at our restaurants.

Your favourite book on wine. The Decline of the Roman Empire.

What country would you visit for its vineyards? England: astonishing that they are producing sparkling close to Champagne quality.

Your favourite champagne.
No offense to the English, but Henriot Cuvée des Enchanteleurs 1996.

If you could drink only one wine for the rest of your life, what would it be?
None. The pleasure of wine is variety, not monogamy.

Your favourite wine quote or motto. See above.

Michel Dovaz

Author of Fine Wines *(Assouline)*

Your first wine memory. *Without a doubt, a chianti.*

Are you Burgundy or Bordeaux? *Bordeaux on even days,*
Burgundy on odd days.

New World or Old World? *More Old World, but not exclusively.*

Your favourite region. *Burgundy.*

The best wine you ever tasted. *Romanée-Conti 1929.*

Your favourite food and wine pairing. *A dry scheurebe with a dill-based appetizer.*

Your favourite winemaker or vineyard. *Those from the Mesnil-sur-Oger commune.*

The most valuable bottle you own. *Latour 1928.*

What wine do you wish you could taste? *It doesn't exist anymore: a white from Coucy-le-Château.*

Your favourite partner in wine. *Cordiality, hedonism, sensuality.*

Restaurant you frequent for its wine list. *La Tour d'Argent (Paris).*

What bottle of wine makes the best hostess gift? *Hermitage La Chapelle 1961 (Jaboulet).*

Every wine collection should include: *Bordeaux, Burgundy (Fr),*
Bardi, Tuscany, Bolgheri (I), Moselle (A),
Toro, Ribera del Duero (S), California (USA).

Your favourite time to enjoy a glass. *Between 11:00 a.m. and noon.*

Your choice aperitif. *Blanc de blancs, brut natural champagne.*

Your favourite book on wine. *Right now, Crus classés du Médoc by*
Eric Bernardin and Pierre Le Hong.

What country would you visit for its vineyards? *Patagonia in Chile.*

Your favourite champagne. *For now, a Salon 1996.*

If you could drink only one wine for the rest of your life, what would it be? *Château Rayas 1998.*

Your favourite wine quote or motto. *"Every taster is right."*

Jay McInerney

Wine columnist for The Wall Street Journal;
novelist, screenwriter, and essayist

Your first wine memory. Almaden pink Chablis on the lawn at Tanglewood, Massachusetts, listening to The Who perform *Tommy*.

Are you Burgundy or Bordeaux? Hate to pick, but have to say Burgundy.

New World or Old World? Old.

Your favourite region. Burgundy.

The best wine you ever tasted. The 1955 La Mission-Haut-Brion back in 1995, when we were both forty years old.

Your favourite food and wine pairing. Condrieu and lobster.

What is your favourite exception to this rule: white with fish, red with meat? Grilled salmon and pinot noir.

Your favourite winemaker or vineyard. Clos des Ducs, Domaine d'Angerville, Volnay.

The most valuable bottle you own. The 1961 Latour.

The most undervalued bottle you own. The 2001 Joh. Jos. Prum Wehlener Sonnenuhr Riesling Spatelese.

What wine do you wish you could taste? The 1945 Romanée-Conti.

Your favourite partner in wine. Julian Barnes.

Restaurant you frequent for its wine list. La Tour d'Argent.

What bottle of wine makes the best hostess gift? Rosé champagne.

Every wine collection should include: Barolo.

Your favourite time to enjoy a glass. After finishing my next novel.

Your favourite wine accessory. A nineteenth-century claret jug I bought in Beaune in the mid-nineties.

Your choice aperitif. Blanc de blancs champagne.

Your best adviser. The sommeliers at my favorite restaurants.

Your favourite book on wine. Kermit Lynch's *Adventures on the Wine Route: A Wine Buyer's Tour of France*.

What country would you visit for its vineyards? South Africa.

Your favourite champagne. Dom Pérignon Rosé.

If you could drink only one wine for the rest of your life, what would it be? DRC Montrachet, if someone else is paying.

Your favourite wine quote or motto. Eat, drink, and remarry.

21

Martine de la Brosse

Co-owner of the Paris-based restaurant L'Ami Louis and Château Louis

Your first wine memory. *It was too long ago! No more memories.*

Are you Burgundy or Bordeaux? *Really, Bordeaux.*

New World or Old World? *More Old World, but not exclusively.*

Your favourite region. *Saint-Émilion.*

The best wine you ever tasted. *Cheval Blanc '47.*

Your favourite food and wine pairing. *Toasted bread, truffles, Haut-Brion.*

What is your favourite exception to this rule: white with fish, red with meat? *Bresse chicken and a Meursault: unforgettable.*

Your favourite winemaker or vineyard. *Stéphane Derenoncourt.*

The most valuable bottle you own. *Petrus 1989.*

The most undervalued bottle you own. *Talbot 1982.*

What wine do you wish you could taste? *A vertical of Le Pin.*

Your favourite partner in wine. *People who make me laugh.*

Restaurant you frequent for its wine list. *Taillevent.*

What bottle of wine makes the best hostess gift? *La Marzelle 2002.*

Every wine collection should include: *2,000-3,000 bottles*

Your favourite time to enjoy a glass. *Before dinner, as an aperitif.*

Your favourite wine accessory. *A very fine crystal glass.*

Your choice aperitif. *The same wine served at dinner.*

Your favourite book on wine. *The Saint-Émilion guide to wine by Henri Enjalbert, and Parker's indispensable book.*

What country would you visit for its vineyards? *The Mendoza region of Argentina.*

Your favourite champagne. *Veuve Clicquot Millésimé.*

If you could drink only one wine for the rest of your life, what would it be? *Château Louis!*

Your favourite wine quote or motto. *If truth is in wine, let it stay there.*

Mario Batali

Chef of Italian cuisine, restaurateur, and cookbook author

Your first wine memory.

Are you Burgundy or Bordeaux? *Burg.*

New World or Old World? *Old.*

Your favourite region. *Montalcino.*

The best wine you ever tasted. *Double mag '45 Cheval Blanc.*

Your favourite food and wine pairing. *Marinated anchovies and Falanghina.*

What is your favourite exception to this rule: white with fish, red with meat? *I love reisling with choucroute, and Taurasi with grilled salmon.*

Your favourite winemaker or vineyard. *J.L. Chave.*

The most valuable bottle you own. *Case of mags of 61 Latour.*

The most undervalued bottle you own.

What wine do you wish you could taste? *All Montrachet by DRC.*

Your favourite partner in wine. *Joe Bastianich.*

Restaurant you frequent for its wine list. *Casa Mono.*

What bottle of wine makes the best hostess gift? *Champagne.*

Every wine collection should include: *Rioja.*

Your favourite time to enjoy a glass. *9:30 pm.*

Your favourite wine accessory. *A glass.*

Your choice aperitif. *Aperol spritz.*

Your best adviser. *Joe Bastianich.*

Your favourite book on wine. *Billionaire's Vinegar.*

What country would you visit for its vineyards? *Italy. Although I do not love wineries, I love vineyards.*

Your favourite champagne. *1985 Dom Pérignon Rosé.*

If you could drink only one wine for the rest of your life, what would it be? *Friulano.*

Your favourite wine quote or motto. *Stop talking about it and taste it.*

Graydon Carter

Editor in chief of Vanity Fair;
co-owner of Monkey Bar and The Waverly Inn

Your first wine memory. *No memory of it exactly, but I do know that I didn't need a corkscrew to open it.*

Are you Burgundy or Bordeaux? *My wife drinks Burgundy, so I've learned to, if not love it, at least appreciate it.*

New World or Old World? *Both, definitely.*

Your favourite region. *I do like California.*

The best wine you ever tasted. *For some reason, good wine always tastes better in restaurants than the same bottle does at home. That said, about 20 years ago, I had a mid-19th-century Lafite Rothschild at Sao Schlumberger's house in Paris that was out of this world.*

Your favourite food and wine pairing. *Just about anything with a bottle of Modicum. But only when I feel relatively flush—it's not cheap.*

What is your favourite exception to this rule: white with fish, red with meat? *I've never been hidebound about red with meat and such. A good bottle of red wine goes well with just about anything including a peanut butter sandwich. In fact, especially with a peanut butter sandwich.*

Your favourite winemaker or vineyard. *Something with Lafite on the label.*

The most valuable bottle you own. *Can't remember the year exactly—but whatever it was, I sold it at Christie's last year.*

The most undervalued bottle you own. *I do like the Robert Mondavi cabernet. And it's generally under $30.*

CHÂTEAU
BORDEAUX
MARGAUX

What wine do you wish you could taste?

Your favourite partner in wine. *Well, my wife, certainly. But also my grown kids.*

Restaurant you frequent for its wine list. *That's easy: The Monkey Bar and The Waverly Inn.*

What bottle of wine makes the best hostess gift? *We generally show up with a bottle of rosé champagne.*

Every wine collection should include: *A bottle of Extra-Strength Tylenol.*

Your favourite time to enjoy a glass. *After the end of a long day at the office. Or at the end of a long day at home. Basically at the end of every day.*

Your favourite wine accessory. *The little corks that expensive Paris hotels give you to re-cork the wine you haven't finished.*

Your choice aperitif. *A Graydon Carter, as served at the American Bar in the Savoy Hotel in London.*

Your best adviser. *Belinda Chang, our manager at The Monkey Bar, and Emil Varda, manager of The Waverly Inn.*

Your favourite book on wine. *The Billionaire's Vinegar.*

What country would you visit for its vineyards? *France.*

Your favourite champagne. *Moët. Or Krug. But I truly love prosecco.*

If you could drink only one wine for the rest of your life, what would it be? *A meaty Californian cabernet.*

Your favourite wine quote or motto. *Soda water or salt are best for getting the stains out.*

Belinda Chang

Wine director at Monkey Bar, in New York City

Your first wine memory. BOTTLE OF LANCERS IN MY PARENTS' REFRIGERATOR...

Are you Burgundy or Bordeaux? BORDEAUX!

New World or Old World? NEW WORLD WITH OLD WORLD SENSIBILITY.

Your favourite region. CHANGES EVERY TWO SECONDS.

The best wine you ever tasted. THE ONE IN MY GLASS RIGHT NOW...

Your favourite food and wine pairing. LATE HARVEST CONDRIEU WITH LOBSTER CAPPUCCINO.

What is your favourite exception to this rule: white with fish, red with meat? COLLIOURE WITH WHITE FISH.

Your favourite winemaker or vineyard. CHANGES EVERY TWO SECONDS.

The most valuable bottle you own. I DON'T OWN ANY VALUABLE BOTTLES, REALLY.

The most undervalued bottle you own. NOTHING IS SACRED. I JUST DRINK THEM.

What wine do you wish you could taste? 1900 BORDEAUX ON RELEASE.

Your favourite partner in wine. GREAT FOOD!

Restaurant you frequent for its wine list. THE ONE THAT I AM WORKING IN.

What bottle of wine makes the best hostess gift? ARMAGNAC.

Every wine collection should include: THE WINES THAT YOU LOVE.

Your favourite time to enjoy a glass. ALWAYS.

Your favourite wine accessory. $5 CORKSCREW.

Your choice aperitif. ANYTHING SPARKLING.

Your best adviser. MYSELF.

Your favourite book on wine. SOTHEBY'S WINE ENCYCLOPEDIA — I GREW UP WITH IT.

What country would you visit for its vineyards? ALL — WINE COUNTRY IS ALWAYS FUN.

Your favourite champagne. SALLY AKA SALON.

If you could drink only one wine for the rest of your life, what would it be? ? THAT'S MEAN.

Your favourite wine quote or motto. RULES ARE MADE TO BE BROKEN.

Philippe Pascal

Owner of the Clos du Cellier aux Moines winery, in Burgundy, France

Your first wine memory. I was seven! To celebrate my age of reason, my dad poured me some cheap red table wine mixed with a lot of tap water! I felt like a REAL MAN ---

Are you Burgundy or Bordeaux? I am BURGUNDY, no question! ... Studied in Dijon, Married in Beaune ... bought an old estate in Givry --- "Je suis fier d'être BOURGUIGNON" famous french drinking song!

New World or Old World? Old World born, but New World CRAZY ... Napa, Anderson, Mendoza, Margaret River, Marlborough county... I even made wine in Bangalore INDIA with famous winemaker Michel Rolland and David Hohnen, founder of Cloudy Bay.

Your favourite region. Burgundy, AGAIN! and again ... I love the history, the cistercian monks, the architecture, the real simple people, the real food, hard winters, warm summers... the stone walls in the country side ---

The best wine you ever tasted. Château d'Yquem 1988 at sunset in the delta of OKAVANGO in BOTSWANA, after 8 hours in the saddle, cantering in the bush ---

Your favourite food and wine pairing. K.I.S.! Pinot noir with BBQ Sirloin & Ribs, Chardonnay with grilled Maine Lobster, Vintage Port with Stilton cheese, Cabernet with bitter chocolate cake ---

What is your favourite exception to this rule: white with fish, red with meat? Red Burgundy served cool* with any white grilled fish, young red Graves (Bordeaux) with fresh oysters. (* cellar temperature)

Your favourite winemaker or vineyard. Richard Geoffroy, Dom Pérignon. A modern monk with a vision, a mission and a great sense of humour.

The most valuable bottle you own. One Magnum of Cheval Blanc 1947... still waiting for the right occasion!?

The most undervalued bottle you own. the "Clos du Cellier aux Moines" Givry 1st growth ... our family estate wine ... so good ... but retailing for only 40 US$ in France.

What wine do you wish you could taste? every vintage of LA ROMANÉE-CONTI of the 20th century ... and possibly the 21st too...

Your favourite partner in wine.
Catherine, my wife, born in Beaune ... she brought me to Burgundy and raised
my wine standards for sure! She manages our wine estate in Givry, small & beautiful ...

Restaurant you frequent for its wine list. L'Ami Louis and LAURENT, in PARIS. Apicius, too ...
Bernard Loiseau in Burgundy.
David Bouley in N.Y.C.
Windows on the World WAS our favorite allar!

What bottle of wine makes the best hostess gift?
Veuve Clicquot Vintage, no hesitation

Every wine collection should include:
Burgundy, Red & whites!

Your favourite time to enjoy a glass bottle.
Sunset, everywhere ...

Your favourite wine accessory. My Old Corkscrew...
Never leaves home without it!

Your choice aperitif. champagne - no alternative

Your best adviser. the Wine Spectator ... and my friend MARVIN S.

Your favourite book on wine. Fine Wines - Best vintages since 1900
by Michel DOVAZ (ed. ASSOULINE)

What country would you visit for its vineyards?
Greece ... where the serious wine world started -

Your favourite champagne. KRUG Reserve. Simply.

If you could drink only one wine for the rest of your life, what would it be? Yquem ...
one sip before falling asleep every night for the rest of my life.

Your favourite wine quote or motto. "Simplex NaturA" latin motto from
the cistercian monks making wine in the XIIIth Century in Burgundy.
"Simply Nature" ... nothing else ... cheers Philippe

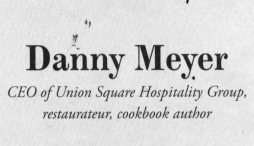

Danny Meyer

CEO of Union Square Hospitality Group,
restaurateur, cookbook author

Your first wine memory. MY FATHER POURING A BOTTLE OF LOUIS JADOT BEAUJOLAIS-VILLAGES OVER A STEAK ON THE GRILL TO DOUSE THE FLAMES.

Are you Burgundy or Bordeaux?
BURGUNDY.

New World or Old World?
OLD WORLD.

Your favourite region.
PIEDMONT.

The best wine you ever tasted. THAT'S NOT FAIR! All taste better when you're with someone you love.

Your favourite food and wine pairing.
QUINTARELLI Amarone with chunks of aged Parmigiano Reggiano.

What is your favourite exception to this rule: white with fish, red with meat?
CHAMPAGNE WITH BARBECUED RIBS.

Your favourite winemaker or vineyard.
GIUSEPPE QUINTARELLI.

The most valuable bottle you own.
1982 CHÂTEAU PETRUS.

The most undervalued bottle you own.
1999 TALENTI BRUNELLO AI MONTALCINO PARETAIO.

What wine do you wish you could taste?
1982 CHÂTEAU PETRUS. IT'S TOO VALUABLE TO OPEN.

Your favourite partner in wine.
MY WIFE, AUDREY.

Restaurant you frequent for its wine list.
MAIALINO, NYC.

What bottle of wine makes the best hostess gift?
SOMETHING YOU WOULD LOVE TO DRINK FOR DINNER YOURSELF.

Every wine collection should include:
LOTS OF BAROLO. YOU NEVER NEED TO RUSH IT.

Your favourite time to enjoy a glass.
SATURDAY NIGHT.

Your favourite wine accessory.
ANY OF OUR DOZEN CORKSCREWS, HAVEN'T FIGURED OUT THE SHOE TRICK!

Your choice aperitif.
BILLECART-SALMON.

Your best adviser.
JANCIS ROBINSON.

Your favourite book on wine.
VICTOR HAZAN'S SEMINAL BOOK ON THE WINES OF ITALY.

What country would you visit for its vineyards?
ALMOST ANY. BUT ITALY TOPS MY LIST.

Your favourite champagne.
BILLECART-SALMON BLANC DE BLANCS.

If you could drink only one wine for the rest of your life, what would it be?
BRICCO MANZONI FROM ROCCHE DEI MANZONI.

Your favourite wine quote or motto.

WINE IS DIVINE. MAKES LIFE SO MUCH BETTER. 33

Daniel Boulud

Chef and restaurateur

Your first wine memory. in my village in France, made
our own wine, Baco Noir varietal, very Tanic, organic,
a bit sour but our own wine.

Are you Burgundy or Bordeaux?

Burgundy everyday! Bordeaux on Sunday!

New World or Old World?

Old world most of the time. New world when i travel.

Your favourite region. Burgundy and Rhône.
Basically a 250 Km radius around Lyon.

The best wine you ever tasted. 1990 Henri Bonneau "cuvée Speciale"
châteauneuf-du-pape
...When terroir creates monster wine!

Your favourite food and wine pairing. Chave Hermitage blanc 1993 with
a crispy calf head stuffed with tongue, Sweetbread and truffle.

What is your favourite exception to this rule: white with fish, red with meat?

a red Burgundy with spiced Salmon baked in Clay, red wine-fig sauce.

Your favourite winemaker or vineyard. Winemaker: besides 10 very good friends in Burgundy----
Jean Louis Chave in Mauve. Rhône
Vineyard: Château Latour and Haut-Brion for
their majestic Location and wine.

The most valuable bottle you own.
I'm not telling, but it's old
and powerful in finesse.

The most undervalued bottle you own.
if i say, the value may go up and then I won't be able to
buy more of it.

What wine do you wish you could taste?
Romanée - Conti 1945.

Your favourite partner in wine. Dean Santon, a passionate
friend who shares the same taste for wine and music.

34

Restaurant you frequent for its wine list. — Bar Boulud, NYC and London, for Burgundy and Rhône.
— Blackberry Farm, Tennessee, for the largest american collection I have seen.

What bottle of wine makes the best hostess gift? anything 1990 from Champagne, Bordeaux, Burgundy, Rhône and California.

Every wine collection should include:
a horizontal of the best vintage
a vertical of the best wine maker.

Your favourite time to enjoy a glass.
at home after work or on Sunday with friends.

Your favourite wine accessory.
— a Riedel collection of carafes and sommelier stemware.

Your choice aperitif. Before dinner: Champagne, Tête de cuvée.
after dinner: more champagne.

Your best adviser.
Daniel Johnnes.

Your favourite book on wine. Jay McInerney
a hedonist in the cellar, adventures in Wine.

What country would you visit for its vineyards? France: All of them.
US: Napa, Oregon, Santa Barbara.
Other: Argentina, South Africa, Australia.

Your favourite champagne.
Dom Pérignon Oenothèque 1996.

If you could drink only one wine for the rest of your life, what would it be?
Château Latour 2000.
Mythical vintage.

Your favourite wine quote or motto.
the rarer the wine, the fewer the friends you need to drink it with.

Daniel Johnnes

Wine director for Daniel Boulud's Dinex Group

Your first wine memory. *I always remember family gatherings with a bottle of Manischewitz on the table.*

Are you Burgundy or Bordeaux? *Ask anyone in the world of wine and they will laugh at the question. BURGUNDY!!!*

New World or Old World? *Old world. My palate was trained on French wine.*

Your favourite region. *Burgundy for its wines and Provence for its natural beauty.*

The best wine you ever tasted. *Henri Jayer Vosne-Romanée 1992 with Henri Jayer in the quiet of his cellar. Not because it is the best wine ever made but because I was tasting a great winemaker with the greatest winemaker ever.*

Your favourite food and wine pairing. *PÂTÉ DE CAMPAGNE with FLEURIE DOMAINE G. ROUMIER, CHAMBOLLE-MUSIGNY LES AMOUREUSES WITH ROASTED BRESSE CHICKEN + CHANTERELLES.*

What is your favourite exception to this rule: white with fish, red with meat?
DANIEL BOULUD'S SALMON BAKED IN CLAY WITH A VOLNAY CLOS DES DUCS FROM D'ANGERVILLE.

Your favourite winemaker or vineyard. *My favorite vineyard on the planet is Musigny and my favorite winemakers are those who can transform grapes from Musigny into liquid dreams - ROUMIER, MUGNIER, DROUHIN, JADOT.*

The most valuable bottle you own. *My wine cellar is filled with bottles that are very valuable for reasons other than market forces. Although I have some bottles worth quite a few dollars, the most valuable have emotional ties, such as my magnum of ROUMIER BONNES-MARES V.V. 1988.*

The most undervalued bottle you own.
1988 MAXIMIN GRÜNHÄUSER ABTSBERG RIESLING AUSLESE FUDER 67.

What wine do you wish you could taste?

CHÂTEAU LAFITE-ROTHSCHILD 1870 MAGNUM FROM GLAMIS CASTLE.

Your favourite partner in wine. *My wife, Sally, is my partner in everything.*

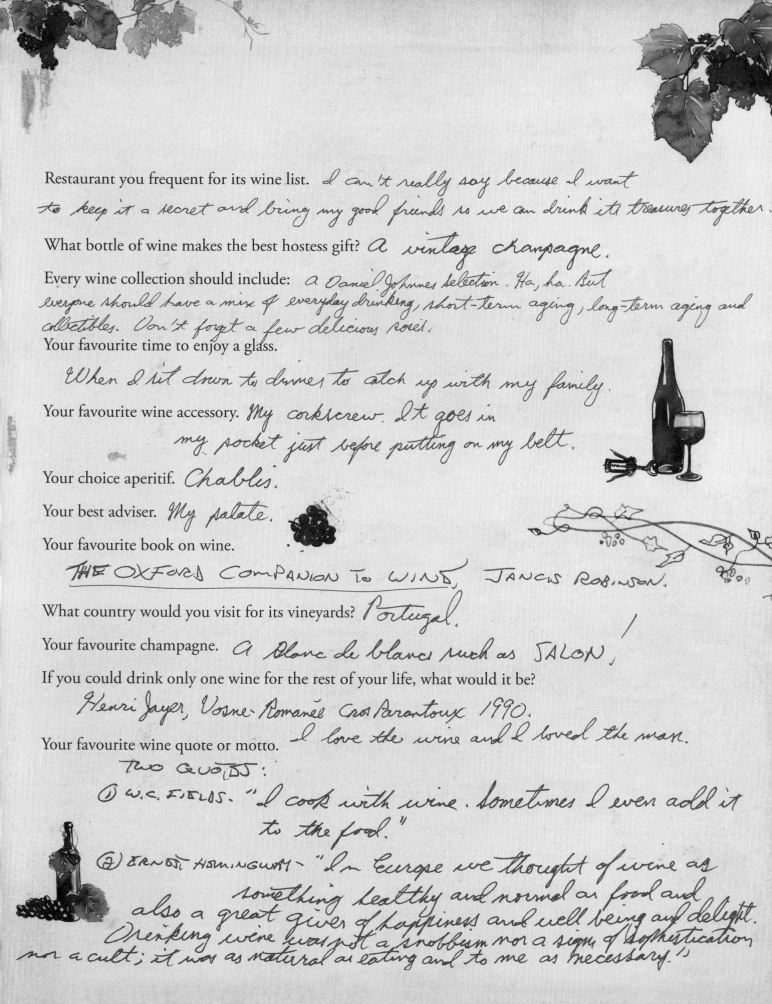

Restaurant you frequent for its wine list. *I can't really say because I want to keep it a secret and bring my good friends so we can drink its treasures together.*

What bottle of wine makes the best hostess gift? *A vintage champagne.*

Every wine collection should include: *A Daniel Johnnes selection. Ha, ha. But everyone should have a mix of everyday drinking, short-term aging, long-term aging and collectibles. Don't forget a few delicious rosés.*

Your favourite time to enjoy a glass.

When I sit down to dinner to catch up with my family.

Your favourite wine accessory. *My corkscrew. It goes in my pocket just before putting on my belt.*

Your choice aperitif. *Chablis.*

Your best adviser. *My palate.*

Your favourite book on wine.

THE OXFORD COMPANION TO WINE, JANCIS ROBINSON.

What country would you visit for its vineyards? *Portugal.*

Your favourite champagne. *A Blanc de blancs such as SALON.*

If you could drink only one wine for the rest of your life, what would it be?

Henri Jayer, Vosne-Romanée Cros Parantoux 1990.

Your favourite wine quote or motto. *I love the wine and I loved the man.*

TWO QUOTES:

① W.C. FIELDS. "I cook with wine. Sometimes I even add it to the food."

② ERNEST HEMINGWAY ~ "In Europe we thought of wine as something healthy and normal as food and also a great giver of happiness and well being and delight. Drinking wine was not a snobbism nor a sign of sophistication nor a cult; it was as natural as eating and to me as necessary."

Benjamin Roffet

Head sommelier of the Trianon Palace, at Versailles;
winner of the Union of French Sommeliers' 2011 award for France's Best Sommelier

Your first wine memory. *A cru from the Rhône valley, without a doubt a CNDP [Châteauneuf-du-Pape].*

Are you Burgundy or Bordeaux? *Personally, I'm Burgundy.*

New World or Old World? *Originally Old World, but culturally New World.*

Your favourite region. *Right now, Central Otago in New Zealand.*

The best wine you ever tasted. *The one I've never tasted!*

Your favourite food and wine pairing. *Indulgent: A Côtes-du-Forez with bacon braised in red wine.*
Classic: A ten-year-old Sauternes with a Chinese Szechuan dish.

Your favourite winemaker or vineyard. *The Loire Valley, for its diversity.*

The most valuable bottle you own. *A bottle from the Château Latour-Martillac,*
from the year I was born.

The most undervalued bottle you own.

What wine do you wish you could taste? *A Henri Jayer Cros Parantoux from the 1980s.*

Your favourite partner in wine. *Several friends.*

Restaurant you frequent for its wine list. *L'Astrance in Paris.*

What bottle of wine makes the best hostess gift? *A good bottle!*

Every wine collection should include: *Good bottles!*

Your favourite time to enjoy a glass. *After work.*

Your favourite wine accessory. *A suitable glass.*

Your choice aperitif. *A blanc de blancs champagne is often the best aperitif.*

Your favourite book on wine. *The Oxford Companion to Wine by Jancis Robinson.*

What country would you visit for its vineyards? *Chile, very soon.*

Your favourite champagne. *For now, Bollinger 2002.*

If you could drink only one wine for the rest of your life, what would it be? *Tokaji cuvée Kapi Disnökö 1999.*

Your favourite wine quote or motto. *"Wine is the healthiest drink." –Pasteur*

Carolyn Wente

Vice chairman of Wente Vineyards

Your first wine memory. *At age 6, tasting sauvignon blancs at the winery with my father and grandfather.*

Are you Burgundy or Bordeaux? *Proudly, I am Californian (I do love Chardonnay & PN).*

New World or Old World? *New World fruit flavors with Old World balance & elegance.*

Your favourite region. *The rolling vineyards of Livermore Valley, California.*

The best wine you ever tasted. *I believe in the wine of the moment, not in better/best.*

Your favourite food and wine pairing. *A classic — Château d'Yquem with sautéed foie gras.*

What is your favourite exception to this rule: white with fish, red with meat? *Beautiful dry rosé with loads of things — a great crossover.*

Your favourite winemaker or vineyard. *Easy! My nephew, Karl Wente, fifth-generation winemaker.*

The most valuable bottle you own. *Invaluable 1995 Wente Vineyards double magnum commemorating my son's birth.*

The most undervalued bottle you own. *Wente Vineyards Riesling, a refreshing wine with versatility.*

What wine do you wish you could taste? *When at its prime, 1787 Château Lafite, owned by Thomas Jefferson.*

Your favourite partner in wine. *My brother Philip, who has an incredible palate and intellect.*

Restaurant you frequent for its wine list. *The wonderful selection of American wines at The Restaurant at Wente Vineyards.*

What bottle of wine makes the best hostess gift? *One that can be opened and does not need cellaring.*

Every wine collection should include: *Several cases of your favorite everyday wines on hand for friends.*

Your favourite time to enjoy a glass. *While I am cooking.*

Your favourite wine accessory. *A classic waiter's corkscrew with a sharp knife.*

Your choice aperitif. *Wente Vineyards Riva Ranch Chardonnay.*

Your best adviser. *My husband, Buck Layton.*

Your favourite book on wine. *Jancis Robinson's The Oxford Companion to Wine.*

What country would you visit for its vineyards? *I have yet to visit New Zealand and am very intrigued.*

Your favourite champagne. *Krug — Tête de Cuvée, Clos d'Ambonnay.*

If you could drink only one wine for the rest of your life, what would it be? *As a varietal, Pinot Noir (Wente Vineyards, of course!).*

Your favourite wine quote or motto. *"Wine is constant proof that God loves us and loves to see us happy." Benjamin Franklin*

Leonid Rath

Co-owner of Lobmeyr

Your first wine memory. *Having a wine chaudeau, a dessert from egg and white wine, that my grandmother used to make us when we were about 8 years old.*

Are you Burgundy or Bordeaux? *If I have to decide, Burgundy.*

New World or Old World? *Old world, preferably from small estates.*

Your favourite region. *Wachau-Kremstal. Romantic place where you can find fabulous white wines.*

The best wine you ever tasted. *A Romanée-Conti La Tache at an exclusive tasting salon in Tokyo.*

Your favourite food and wine pairing. *Foie gras with a nice riesling grand cru.*

What is your favourite exception to this rule: white with fish, red with meat? *Venison with a Château Grillet.*

Your favourite winemaker or vineyard. *www.heinrich.at—Wide range, good quality, fair price.*

The most valuable bottle you own. *A red from my cousin-in-law's vineyard—a gift for our daughter's birth.*

The most undervalued bottle you own. *Pinot noir Dankbarkeit 2007 by Josef Lentsch Podersdorf-Burgenland.*

What wine do you wish you could taste? *The best wines of the Roman Empire. There must have been some good ones around.*

Your favourite partner in wine. *www.ungerundklein.at.*

Restaurant you frequent for its wine list. *www.kimkocht.at.*

What bottle of wine makes the best hostess gift? *I don't give wine, I give glasses.*

Every wine collection should include: *Wiener Gemischter Satz, a special blend from Vienna that has been admitted to the Slow Food Foundation's Ark of Taste.*

Your favourite time to enjoy a glass. *When the kids are in bed.*

Your favourite wine accessory. *Lobmeyr Ballerina red wine tasting glass.*

Your choice aperitif. *Champagne (blanc de blancs extra brut).*

Your best adviser. *Mr. Shimura, our Japanese importer.*

Your favourite book on wine. *The Taste of Wine: The Art and Science of Wine Appreciation, by Emile Peynaud.*

What country would you visit for its vineyards? *South Tyrol in autumn.*

Your favourite champagne. *Brut terroir (blanc de blancs), found on www.champagne-agrapart.com.*

If you could drink only one wine for the rest of your life, what would it be? *Grüner Veltliner.*

Your favourite wine quote or motto. *Wine is bottled poetry.*

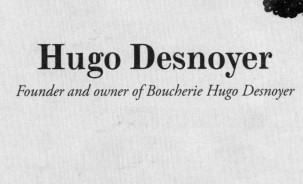

Hugo Desnoyer

Founder and owner of Boucherie Hugo Desnoyer

Your first wine memory. *In my opinion, in my mother's womb.*

Are you Burgundy or Bordeaux? *Burgundy!!!*

New World or Old World? *Old World...*

Your favourite region. *Vosne-Romanée.*

The best wine you ever tasted. *Clos de Bèze 1999 Prieuré Roch.*

Your favourite food and wine pairing. *Milk-fed veal with Chambolle.*

What is your favourite exception to this rule: white with fish, red with meat?

Your favourite winemaker or vineyard. *René Mosse.*

The most valuable bottle you own. *Romanée-Conti.*

The most undervalued bottle you own.

What wine do you wish you could taste? *A very delicate pinot noir...*

Your favourite partner in wine. *Stéphane Sifres.*

Restaurant you frequent for its wine list. *Jean-Michel Lorain in Joigny.*

What bottle of wine makes the best hostess gift? *Hautes Mézève 1997 Prieuré Roch.*

Every wine collection should include: *Pinot noir!*

Your favourite time to enjoy a glass. *Late afternoon.*

Your favourite wine accessory. *A corkscrew / a Spiegelau glass.*

Your choice aperitif. *René Mosse, Terres Blanches.*

Your best adviser. *Stéphane Sifres.*

Your favourite book on wine. *L'Atlas des grands vignobles de Bourgogne.*

What country would you visit for its vineyards? *South Africa.*

Your favourite champagne. *Selosse.*

If you could drink only one wine for the rest of your life, what would it be? *Denis Mortet.*

Your favourite wine quote or motto. *Bottles of wine are like women—they're all different.*

Joël Robuchon

Chef at the Atelier Étoile de Joël Robuchon and
the Atelier Saint-Germain de Jöel Robuchon restaurants, in Paris

Your first wine memory. It was in the 1950s when I was a little boy. In church, I was responsible for the bread and wine for the Eucharist. I remember that it was a white wine—light and pleasant. Hopefully God will forgive me....

Are you Burgundy or Bordeaux? I love all wines, as long as they aren't too acidic. I believe that wine should accompany a meal. Certain dishes go with a Bordeaux, others with a Burgundy. My friend Bernard Magrez introduced me to some white Bordeaux wines that I loved, the Château Pape Clément or the white Bordeaux from Château Fonbrauge. I think that a lot of white Bordeaux are wrongly forgotten.

New World or Old World? The origins of a wine aren't very important to me. I'm not a strict rule-follower. If I like a wine, I wouldn't change my mind about it because of its place of production.

Your favourite region. I love the Côtes du Rhône, especially Châteauneuf-du-Pape.

The best wine you ever tasted. Mr. Alan Ho, the owner of the Grand Lisboa hotel in Macau, is the best wine connoisseur in the world and a big collector of prestigious bottles. It's thanks to him that I was able to taste some wines from my birth year (1945), like the Château Mouton Rothschild, Château Lafleur, Château Latour, Petrus, Château d'Yquem...

Your favourite food and wine pairing. It was during my vacation in Spain. The wonderful paella from Paco Gandia in Spain combined with a jumilla, a wine from the Murcia region.

Your favourite winemaker or vineyard. As I said earlier, I really like the Châteauneuf-du-Pape, with a preference for Château Rayas. But Château de Beaucastel is equally extraordinary.

The most valuable bottle you own. A blessed bottle of wine that my favorite sommelier, Antoine Hernandez, brought me back from Lourdes.

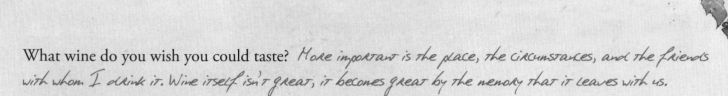

What wine do you wish you could taste? *More important is the place, the circumstances, and the friends with whom I drink it. Wine itself isn't great, it becomes great by the memory that it leaves with us.*

Your favourite partner in wine. *Mr. Alan Ho from Macau.*

Restaurant you frequent for its wine list. *Robuchon à Galera, in Macau.*

What bottle of wine makes the best hostess gift? *You have to know what their tastes and preferences are!!!*

Every wine collection should include: *Several bottles from Languedoc-Roussillon, which currently has the best quality/price ratings in France.*

Your favourite time to enjoy a glass. *Before or during a meal. I don't drink wine outside of meals.*

Your favourite wine accessory. *A corkscrew from Laguiole that Antoine Hernandez brought back for me from Lourdes.*

Your choice aperitif. *Champagne.*

Your favourite book on wine. *Le Monde du vin: Art ou bluff, by my friend Guy Renvoisé.*

What country would you visit for its vineyards? *I don't know... I'd like to know the lesser-known places in wonderful countries, but also where gastronomy and wine are supreme: France.*

Your favourite champagne. *Bruno Paillard champagne.*

If you could drink only one wine for the rest of your life, what would it be? *An excellent wine produced in big quantities, because I don't intend to die anytime soon!*

Your favourite wine quote or motto. *"Wine is the healthiest and the most hygienic of drinks." -Pasteur*

Bernard Burtschy

Wine critic for Le Figaro, La Revue du Vin de France, *and* L'Amateur de cigare

Your first wine memory. *Despite coming from a modest background, or maybe thanks to it, I was lucky enough to be continually introduced to gastronomy and wine, but never to a particular wine. However, I do remember the first wine that I drank in a nice restaurant with my first real salary in 1974: It was a Pomerol, Château Rouget 1964, at the mythic Lasserre.*

Are you Burgundy or Bordeaux? *There are so many wonderful regions in France and throughout the entire world. I'm too young—I haven't tried enough wines. I need to continue creating options for myself...*

New World or Old World? *I don't have a preference. Wherever great wines are produced, I feel at home.*

Your favourite region. *There are so many, but I have a slight weakness for my region, Alsace.*

The best wine you ever tasted. *A lot of wines come to mind. Maybe Clos de Vougeot 1965 from Bouchard Père et Fils. At the time, Clos de Vougeot only had one proprietor and I never thought—even in my craziest dreams—that I would be able to drink such a wonderful Clos de Vougeot.*

Your favourite food and wine pairing. *Hare à la royale (the senator's recipe) with a red Hermitage.*

Your favourite winemaker or vineyard. *Alsace and Burgundy, for the richness of their terrain.*

The most valuable bottle you own. *There are a lot, taking into account that value for me isn't so much the price, but the feeling something gives me. Chambertin Clos de Bèze 1921, from an unknown producer, black as ink, indestructible and sublime.*

What wine do you wish you could taste? *Château d'Yquem 1811, the year of the comet.*

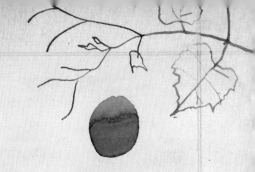

Your favourite partner in wine. *A lover of wine and good food, someone who knows how to eat and drink, which is becoming more and more rare these days.*

Restaurant you frequent for its wine list. *The Alsatian tavern in Ingersheim, in Alsace.*

What bottle of wine makes the best hostess gift? *One from their birth year.*

Every wine collection should include: *A little bit of everything, well-known and lesser-known bottles.*

Your favourite time to enjoy a glass. *At every daytime and nighttime hour.*

Your favourite wine accessory. *A carafe, to be handled with care.*

Your choice aperitif. *A good champagne.*

Your favourite book on wine. *Raymond Dumay's wine guide. The appellations are a little outdated, but it's still relevant. And he's so right.*

What country would you visit for its vineyards? *All of them. Luckily, there are only a few that I still need to visit, such as New Zealand.*

Your favourite champagne. *Why only one? Krug, Bollinger, Salon, Dom Pérignon, Comtes de Champagne, among many others.*

If you could drink only one wine for the rest of your life, what would it be?
I hope that I'll never have to deal with this dramatic situation. There are so many good wines, and so many more to discover.

Your favourite wine quote or motto. *"Within the bottle's depths, the wine's soul sang one night." —Baudelaire*

Jean-Charles Boisset

President of Boisset Family Estates

Your first wine memory. I was 7 years old & had the lovely & delightful home task to set the table, crust to table and prepare the wine for my parents... I was observing my adorable mother all night long, looking at the wine color, feeling the bouquet and taste in small sips the elixir of god... As they retired to another salon, I imitated her, as a boy admiring his mom, and tasted all her glasses which were still full... I started to feel the emotions, sensations and passion for wine, to the point that I had vertigo and went up to my room... The rest is history!

This gave birth to my #7!

Are you Burgundy or Bordeaux?

Burgundy,
for its sensual, emotional, intense and delicate touch, and grandiose finish!

New World or Old World? Both, I created a perfect wine recently, N°3... the Burgundy, Sonoma = 3 not 2... As both worlds are the most fabulous to associate, marry and forever cherish...

Your favourite region.
Côte de Nuits in Burgundy, with a touch of of Sonoma, Russian River of course!

The best wine you ever tasted. It was with my irresistible wife, on our engagement... It was for her of course... A Charmes Chambertin grand cru... Domaine de la Vougeraie!

Your favourite food and wine pairing.
- Caviar with Crémant de Bourgogne JCB # #69,
- Foie gras with Clos de Vougeot Blanc Vougeraie.
- Smoked salmon with BV Sta Carneros Chardonnay
- Lapin à la moutarde with DeLoach green Valley.
- Cheeses from CA / France with Raymond generations
- Apple pie with L. Bouillot Grand terroir sparkling

What is your favourite exception to this rule: white with fish, red with meat?
My favourites: Trout with Pinot Noir
Beef with Cabernet Sauvignon
Goat cheese with Chardonnay

The most valuable bottle you own. The wine goddess (my wife) and I made for our wedding called: Maritas... a blend of her Gallo Pinot Noir Sonoma Vineyards and my JCBoisset Burgundy Côte de Nuits... An Eternal Treasure to drink with a Teaspoon!... and French kisses!!!

The most undervalued bottle you own.
Like a great individual or personality, you are never sure of its evolution!... Most likely, the first wine I had the pleasure to help make ...I was 11 years old... It is a 1980... we will see!!!

What wine do you wish you could taste? A World Blend... I feel all cultures together could create the perfect blend...

Your favourite partner in wine. My Lovely sister, we have been together since birth and she represents all the facets of the most beautiful wines... with even more style for the senses!

Restaurant you frequent for its wine list. Loiseau... in Beaune... or my Mother's house... one of the Best Tables in the World!

What bottle of wine makes the best hostess gift?
JCB #21, the association of Chardonnay & Pinot... en plus... with Bubbles... s'il vous plaît! Mysterious & Flamboyant!

Every wine collection should include: France and America!... "Oceans May Separate us, wine brings us together!"

Your favourite time to enjoy a glass.
7 PM... when I kiss my Lady's "Jumelles" to bed... The most exhilirating Moment!

Your favourite wine accessory. The thief... Love to penetrate the barrel opening to discover the evolution of the vintage...

Your choice aperitif. Bubble, Crémant de Bourgogne... of Course!
#21 in honour of Bourgogne or
#69 ... for whatever it can bring to the party!

Your favourite book on wine. The one which has not yet been written!

What country would you visit for its vineyards? California... In addition to its Vineyards, its incredible and breathtaking buccolic landscape!

Your favourite champagne. It is #69 by JCB... not a champagne, a fraction of the cost ... and so erotic!

If you could drink only one wine for the rest of your life, what would it be?
The wine given and I are creating for our 5-month-old twin girls... a wine with personality, character, strong identity and so feminine that you always with you had ... More! ... what a surprise!

Your favourite wine quote or motto.
"The more I taste wine, the less I know!"
↳ True quote = JCB!

Lamberto Frescobaldi

Vice president of Marchesi de' Frescobaldi

Your first wine memory. *Very young boy in Nipozzano.*

Are you Burgundy or Bordeaux? *I am a burgundy a Bordeaux a Brunello, a Bolgheri a Chianti ....!*

New World or Old World? *the young spirit of the old world.*

Your favourite region. *Tuscany. Some doubt?*

The best wine you ever tasted. *I am working on that. Maybe one day I'll know.*

Your favourite food and wine pairing.
A T-bone from our chianine cows raised in Nipozzano with a glass of Mormoreto 99.

What is your favourite exception to this rule: white with fish, red with meat?
Our Red Mormoreto w/ Monkfish cooked w/ Tomato and black olives.

Your favourite winemaker or vineyard.
My favourite vineyard is the Luce brunello in Montalcino.

The most valuable bottle you own.
a 1961 Nipozzano bottled for my birth.

The most undervalued bottle you own.
many, I have many of them.

What wine do you wish you could taste?
the latest vintage of Le Pin —

Your favourite partner in wine.
My wife, Eleonora.

Restaurant you frequent for its wine list.

L' Enoteca Marcucci. Santa Pietra. Tuscany —

What bottle of wine makes the best hostess gift? Castelgiocondo Brunello di Montalcino
Riserva 2001 —

Every wine collection should include: A couple of vintages of Mormoreto.

Your favourite time to enjoy a glass. Dinner Time w/ friends —

Your favourite wine accessory. Corkscrew +ooooo

Your choice aperitif.
Pomino Benefizio — a terrific Chardonnay.

Your best adviser.
My wife, Eleonora.

Your favourite book on wine.
the sotheby's wine encyclopedia.

What country would you visit for its vineyards?
South Africa — Stellenbosch.

Your favourite champagne.
André Clouet. a Bouzy.

If you could drink only one wine for the rest of your life, what would it be?
Our Remole — Toscana.

Your favourite wine quote or motto. Life is too short to drink bad wine.

Lamberto Frescobaldi.
OCT 19. 2011 —

53

Massimo Bottura

Chef at Osteria Francescana, in Modena, Italy

Your first wine memory. *I will never forget the glass of Barolo Monfortino I drank at Cantarelli, a very famous small osteria outside of Parma. I was on my first gourmet outing with my older brothers. We ate culatello and egg pasta, but the memory of the wine remained. Then and there I decided to start educating myself about food and wine. It was the beginning of everything. Cantarelli no longer exists, but it will always be there in my mind.*

Are you Burgundy or Bordeaux? *Burgundy.*

New World or Old World? *Old World.*

Your favourite region. *Emilia—Romagna, in Italy.*

The best wine you ever tasted. *The next one.*

Your favourite food and wine pairing. *From my backyard: Parmigiano Reggiano with Lambrusco di Modena. An exceptional Parmigiano goes with anything, but to remain within our territory, I would choose to drink an exceptional Lambrusco alongside it.*

From under 100 kilometers: culatello di Zibello, produced and aged by Massimo Spigaroli, along with a glass of Ca' del Bosco Cuvée Annamaria Clementi from Franciacorta, made by my dear friend Maurizio Zanella.

What is your favourite exception to this rule: white with fish, red with meat? *White Timorasso by Walter Massa and suckling pig with crispy skin.*

Your favourite winemaker or vineyard. *Christian Bellei, a local hero who has given Lambrusco nobility and grace.*

The most valuable bottle you own. *I have a bottle of traditional balsamic vinegar from 1872.*

The most undervalued bottle you own. *I still have shards of a bottle of Krug '88 broken by my maître d Beppe Palmieri.*

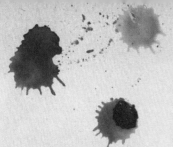

What wine do you wish you could taste? Someday I would like to taste the Lambrusco di Modena that is prized as the best Italian sparkling wine.

Your favourite partner in wine. Lara, my partner in life.

Restaurant you frequent for its wine list. Dal Pescatore, Canneto sull'Oglio, Mantova, run by the Santini family.

What bottle of wine makes the best hostess gift? Something that belongs to your country and your heritage. I usually choose unexpected wines from Emilia-Romagna, such as wines from La Tosa made by Stefano Pizzamiglio. Il Sorriso del Cielo (Smile from the Sky) is a wonderful Malvasia with a beautiful label and name. Unforgettable.

Every wine collection should include: Haut-Brion '89

Your favourite time to enjoy a glass. During Christmas Eve dinner, with my extended family of 24.

Your favourite wine accessory. Willsberger-designed glasses.

Your choice aperitif. A glass of the Beltane Microbrewery made with smoked chestnut.

Your best adviser. The guy who broke the Krug '88 bottle.

Your favourite book on wine. Vino al vino by Mario Soldati.

What country would you visit for its vineyards? I usually visit countries for the people. Having personal experiences is the only way to travel; everything takes on a new light when you add a face to a memory, and especially to a glass of wine.

Your favourite champagne. Clos du Mesnil Krug.

If you could drink only one wine for the rest of your life, what would it be? Dom Pérignon. It runs through my blood like Parmigiano Reggiano and aceto balsamico. Some things can never change.

Your favourite wine quote or motto. "A man does not age, but mellows like fine wine." (I am still waiting for that to happen to me...)

55

Your first wine memory. _____

Are you Burgundy or Bordeaux? _____

New World or Old World? _____

Your favourite region. _____

The best wine you ever tasted. _____

Your favourite food and wine pairing. _____

What is your favourite exception to this rule: white with fish, red with meat? _____

Your favourite winemaker or vineyard. _____

The most valuable bottle you own. _____

The most undervalued bottle you own. _____

What wine do you wish you could taste? _____

Your favourite partner in wine. _____

Restaurant you frequent for its wine list. _____

What bottle of wine makes the best hostess gift? _____

Every wine collection should include: _____

Your favourite time to enjoy a glass. _____

Your favourite wine accessory. _____

Your choice aperitif. _____

Your best adviser. _____

Your favourite book on wine. _____

What country would you visit for its vineyards? _____

Your favourite champagne. _____

If you could drink only one wine for the rest of your life, what would it be? _____

Your favourite wine quote or motto. _____

Your first wine memory. _____

Are you Burgundy or Bordeaux? _____

New World or Old World? _____

Your favourite region. _____

The best wine you ever tasted. _____

Your favourite food and wine pairing. _____

What is your favourite exception to this rule: white with fish, red with meat? _____

Your favourite winemaker or vineyard. _____

The most valuable bottle you own. _____

The most undervalued bottle you own. _____

What wine do you wish you could taste? _____

Your favourite partner in wine. _____

Restaurant you frequent for its wine list. _____

What bottle of wine makes the best hostess gift? _____

Every wine collection should include: _____

Your favourite time to enjoy a glass. _____

Your favourite wine accessory. _____

Your choice aperitif. _____

Your best adviser. _____

Your favourite book on wine. _____

What country would you visit for its vineyards? _____

Your favourite champagne. _____

If you could drink only one wine for the rest of your life, what would it be? _____

Your favourite wine quote or motto. _____

Your first wine memory.

Are you Burgundy or Bordeaux?

New World or Old World?

Your favourite region.

The best wine you ever tasted.

Your favourite food and wine pairing.

What is your favourite exception to this rule: white with fish, red with meat?

Your favourite winemaker or vineyard.

The most valuable bottle you own.

The most undervalued bottle you own.

What wine do you wish you could taste?

Your favourite partner in wine.

Restaurant you frequent for its wine list.

What bottle of wine makes the best hostess gift?

Every wine collection should include:

Your favourite time to enjoy a glass.

Your favourite wine accessory.

Your choice aperitif.

Your best adviser.

Your favourite book on wine.

What country would you visit for its vineyards?

Your favourite champagne.

If you could drink only one wine for the rest of your life, what would it be?

Your favourite wine quote or motto.

60

Your first wine memory. _____

Are you Burgundy or Bordeaux? _____

New World or Old World? _____

Your favourite region. _____

The best wine you ever tasted. _____

Your favourite food and wine pairing. _____

What is your favourite exception to this rule: white with fish, red with meat? _____

Your favourite winemaker or vineyard. _____

The most valuable bottle you own. _____

The most undervalued bottle you own. _____

What wine do you wish you could taste? _____

Your favourite partner in wine. _____

Restaurant you frequent for its wine list. _____

What bottle of wine makes the best hostess gift? _____

Every wine collection should include: _____

Your favourite time to enjoy a glass. _____

Your favourite wine accessory. _____

Your choice aperitif. _____

Your best adviser. _____

Your favourite book on wine. _____

What country would you visit for its vineyards? _____

Your favourite champagne. _____

If you could drink only one wine for the rest of your life, what would it be? _____

Your favourite wine quote or motto. _____

Your first wine memory. _____

Are you Burgundy or Bordeaux? _____

New World or Old World? _____

Your favourite region. _____

The best wine you ever tasted. _____

Your favourite food and wine pairing. _____

What is your favourite exception to this rule: white with fish, red with meat? _____

Your favourite winemaker or vineyard. _____

The most valuable bottle you own. _____

The most undervalued bottle you own. _____

What wine do you wish you could taste? _____

Your favourite partner in wine. _____

Restaurant you frequent for its wine list. _____

What bottle of wine makes the best hostess gift? _____

Every wine collection should include: _____

Your favourite time to enjoy a glass. _____

Your favourite wine accessory. _____

Your choice aperitif. _____

Your best adviser. _____

Your favourite book on wine. _____

What country would you visit for its vineyards? _____

Your favourite champagne. _____

If you could drink only one wine for the rest of your life, what would it be? _____

Your favourite wine quote or motto. _____

Your first wine memory. _____

Are you Burgundy or Bordeaux? _____

New World or Old World? _____

Your favourite region. _____

The best wine you ever tasted. _____

Your favourite food and wine pairing. _____

What is your favourite exception to this rule: white with fish, red with meat? ____

Your favourite winemaker or vineyard. _____

The most valuable bottle you own. _____

The most undervalued bottle you own. _____

What wine do you wish you could taste? _____

Your favourite partner in wine. _____

Restaurant you frequent for its wine list. _____

What bottle of wine makes the best hostess gift? _____

Every wine collection should include: _____

Your favourite time to enjoy a glass. _____

Your favourite wine accessory. _____

Your choice aperitif. _____

Your best adviser. _____

Your favourite book on wine. _____

What country would you visit for its vineyards? _____

Your favourite champagne. _____

If you could drink only one wine for the rest of your life, what would it be? ____

Your favourite wine quote or motto. _____

Your first wine memory. _____

Are you Burgundy or Bordeaux? _____

New World or Old World? _____

Your favourite region. _____

The best wine you ever tasted. _____

Your favourite food and wine pairing. _____

What is your favourite exception to this rule: white with fish, red with meat? _____

Your favourite winemaker or vineyard. _____

The most valuable bottle you own. _____

The most undervalued bottle you own. _____

What wine do you wish you could taste? _____

Your favourite partner in wine. _____

Restaurant you frequent for its wine list. _____

What bottle of wine makes the best hostess gift? _____

Every wine collection should include: _____

Your favourite time to enjoy a glass. _____

Your favourite wine accessory. _____

Your choice aperitif. _____

Your best adviser. _____

Your favourite book on wine. _____

What country would you visit for its vineyards? _____

Your favourite champagne. _____

If you could drink only one wine for the rest of your life, what would it be? _____

Your favourite wine quote or motto. _____

Your first wine memory. _____

Are you Burgundy or Bordeaux? _____

New World or Old World? _____

Your favourite region. _____

The best wine you ever tasted. _____

Your favourite food and wine pairing. _____

What is your favourite exception to this rule: white with fish, red with meat? _____

Your favourite winemaker or vineyard. _____

The most valuable bottle you own. _____

The most undervalued bottle you own. _____

What wine do you wish you could taste? _____

Your favourite partner in wine. _____

Restaurant you frequent for its wine list. _____

What bottle of wine makes the best hostess gift? _____

Every wine collection should include: _____

Your favourite time to enjoy a glass. _____

Your favourite wine accessory. _____

Your choice aperitif. _____

Your best adviser. _____

Your favourite book on wine. _____

What country would you visit for its vineyards? _____

Your favourite champagne. _____

If you could drink only one wine for the rest of your life, what would it be? _____

Your favourite wine quote or motto. _____

Your first wine memory. _____

Are you Burgundy or Bordeaux? _____

New World or Old World? _____

Your favourite region. _____

The best wine you ever tasted. _____

Your favourite food and wine pairing. _____

What is your favourite exception to this rule: white with fish, red with meat? ____

Your favourite winemaker or vineyard. _____

The most valuable bottle you own. _____

The most undervalued bottle you own. _____

What wine do you wish you could taste? _____

Your favourite partner in wine. _____

Restaurant you frequent for its wine list. _____

What bottle of wine makes the best hostess gift? _____

Every wine collection should include: _____

Your favourite time to enjoy a glass. _____

Your favourite wine accessory. _____

Your choice aperitif. _____

Your best adviser. _____

Your favourite book on wine. _____

What country would you visit for its vineyards? _____

Your favourite champagne. _____

If you could drink only one wine for the rest of your life, what would it be? _____

Your favourite wine quote or motto. _____

Your first wine memory.

Are you Burgundy or Bordeaux?

New World or Old World?

Your favourite region.

The best wine you ever tasted.

Your favourite food and wine pairing.

What is your favourite exception to this rule: white with fish, red with meat?

Your favourite winemaker or vineyard.

The most valuable bottle you own.

The most undervalued bottle you own.

What wine do you wish you could taste?

Your favourite partner in wine.

Restaurant you frequent for its wine list.

What bottle of wine makes the best hostess gift?

Every wine collection should include:

Your favourite time to enjoy a glass.

Your favourite wine accessory.

Your choice aperitif.

Your best adviser.

Your favourite book on wine.

What country would you visit for its vineyards?

Your favourite champagne.

If you could drink only one wine for the rest of your life, what would it be?

Your favourite wine quote or motto.

Your first wine memory. _____

Are you Burgundy or Bordeaux? _____

New World or Old World? _____

Your favourite region. _____

The best wine you ever tasted. _____

Your favourite food and wine pairing. _____

What is your favourite exception to this rule: white with fish, red with meat? _____

Your favourite winemaker or vineyard. _____

The most valuable bottle you own. _____

The most undervalued bottle you own. _____

What wine do you wish you could taste? _____

Your favourite partner in wine. _____

Restaurant you frequent for its wine list. _____

What bottle of wine makes the best hostess gift? _____

Every wine collection should include: _____

Your favourite time to enjoy a glass. _____

Your favourite wine accessory. _____

Your choice aperitif. _____

Your best adviser. _____

Your favourite book on wine. _____

What country would you visit for its vineyards? _____

Your favourite champagne. _____

If you could drink only one wine for the rest of your life, what would it be? _____

Your favourite wine quote or motto. _____

Your first wine memory. _____

Are you Burgundy or Bordeaux? _____

New World or Old World? _____

Your favourite region. _____

The best wine you ever tasted. _____

Your favourite food and wine pairing. _____

What is your favourite exception to this rule: white with fish, red with meat? ____

Your favourite winemaker or vineyard. _____

The most valuable bottle you own. _____

The most undervalued bottle you own. _____

What wine do you wish you could taste? _____

Your favourite partner in wine. _____

Restaurant you frequent for its wine list. _____

What bottle of wine makes the best hostess gift? _____

Every wine collection should include: _____

Your favourite time to enjoy a glass. _____

Your favourite wine accessory. _____

Your choice aperitif. _____

Your best adviser. _____

Your favourite book on wine. _____

What country would you visit for its vineyards? _____

Your favourite champagne. _____

If you could drink only one wine for the rest of your life, what would it be? _____

Your favourite wine quote or motto. _____

Your first wine memory.

Are you Burgundy or Bordeaux?

New World or Old World?

Your favourite region.

The best wine you ever tasted.

Your favourite food and wine pairing.

What is your favourite exception to this rule: white with fish, red with meat?

Your favourite winemaker or vineyard.

The most valuable bottle you own.

The most undervalued bottle you own.

What wine do you wish you could taste?

Your favourite partner in wine.

Restaurant you frequent for its wine list.

What bottle of wine makes the best hostess gift?

Every wine collection should include:

Your favourite time to enjoy a glass.

Your favourite wine accessory.

Your choice aperitif.

Your best adviser.

Your favourite book on wine.

What country would you visit for its vineyards?

Your favourite champagne.

If you could drink only one wine for the rest of your life, what would it be?

Your favourite wine quote or motto.

Your first wine memory. _____

Are you Burgundy or Bordeaux? _____

New World or Old World? _____

Your favourite region. _____

The best wine you ever tasted. _____

Your favourite food and wine pairing. _____

What is your favourite exception to this rule: white with fish, red with meat? _____

Your favourite winemaker or vineyard. _____

The most valuable bottle you own. _____

The most undervalued bottle you own. _____

What wine do you wish you could taste? _____

Your favourite partner in wine. _____

Restaurant you frequent for its wine list. _____

What bottle of wine makes the best hostess gift? _____

Every wine collection should include: _____

Your favourite time to enjoy a glass. _____

Your favourite wine accessory. _____

Your choice aperitif. _____

Your best adviser. _____

Your favourite book on wine. _____

What country would you visit for its vineyards? _____

Your favourite champagne. _____

If you could drink only one wine for the rest of your life, what would it be? _____

Your favourite wine quote or motto. _____

Your first wine memory. _____

Are you Burgundy or Bordeaux? _____

New World or Old World? _____

Your favourite region. _____

The best wine you ever tasted. _____

Your favourite food and wine pairing. _____

What is your favourite exception to this rule: white with fish, red with meat? _____

Your favourite winemaker or vineyard. _____

The most valuable bottle you own. _____

The most undervalued bottle you own. _____

What wine do you wish you could taste? _____

Your favourite partner in wine. _____

Restaurant you frequent for its wine list. _____

What bottle of wine makes the best hostess gift? _____

Every wine collection should include: _____

Your favourite time to enjoy a glass. _____

Your favourite wine accessory. _____

Your choice aperitif. _____

Your best adviser. _____

Your favourite book on wine. _____

What country would you visit for its vineyards? _____

Your favourite champagne. _____

If you could drink only one wine for the rest of your life, what would it be? _____

Your favourite wine quote or motto. _____

Your first wine memory. _____

Are you Burgundy or Bordeaux? _____

New World or Old World? _____

Your favourite region. _____

The best wine you ever tasted. _____

Your favourite food and wine pairing. _____

What is your favourite exception to this rule: white with fish, red with meat? _____

Your favourite winemaker or vineyard. _____

The most valuable bottle you own. _____

The most undervalued bottle you own. _____

What wine do you wish you could taste? _____

Your favourite partner in wine. _____

Restaurant you frequent for its wine list. _____

What bottle of wine makes the best hostess gift? _____

Every wine collection should include: _____

Your favourite time to enjoy a glass. _____

Your favourite wine accessory. _____

Your choice aperitif. _____

Your best adviser. _____

Your favourite book on wine. _____

What country would you visit for its vineyards? _____

Your favourite champagne. _____

If you could drink only one wine for the rest of your life, what would it be? _____

Your favourite wine quote or motto. _____

Your first wine memory. _____

Are you Burgundy or Bordeaux? _____

New World or Old World? _____

Your favourite region. _____

The best wine you ever tasted. _____

Your favourite food and wine pairing. _____

What is your favourite exception to this rule: white with fish, red with meat? _____

Your favourite winemaker or vineyard. _____

The most valuable bottle you own. _____

The most undervalued bottle you own. _____

What wine do you wish you could taste? _____

Your favourite partner in wine. _____

Restaurant you frequent for its wine list. _____

What bottle of wine makes the best hostess gift? _____

Every wine collection should include: _____

Your favourite time to enjoy a glass. _____

Your favourite wine accessory. _____

Your choice aperitif. _____

Your best adviser. _____

Your favourite book on wine. _____

What country would you visit for its vineyards? _____

Your favourite champagne. _____

If you could drink only one wine for the rest of your life, what would it be? _____

Your favourite wine quote or motto. _____

Your first wine memory. _____

Are you Burgundy or Bordeaux? _____

New World or Old World? _____

Your favourite region. _____

The best wine you ever tasted. _____

Your favourite food and wine pairing. _____

What is your favourite exception to this rule: white with fish, red with meat? _____

Your favourite winemaker or vineyard. _____

The most valuable bottle you own. _____

The most undervalued bottle you own. _____

What wine do you wish you could taste? _____

Your favourite partner in wine. _____

Restaurant you frequent for its wine list. _____

What bottle of wine makes the best hostess gift? _____

Every wine collection should include: _____

Your favourite time to enjoy a glass. _____

Your favourite wine accessory. _____

Your choice aperitif. _____

Your best adviser. _____

Your favourite book on wine. _____

What country would you visit for its vineyards? _____

Your favourite champagne. _____

If you could drink only one wine for the rest of your life, what would it be? _____

Your favourite wine quote or motto. _____

Your first wine memory. _____

Are you Burgundy or Bordeaux? _____

New World or Old World? _____

Your favourite region. _____

The best wine you ever tasted. _____

Your favourite food and wine pairing. _____

What is your favourite exception to this rule: white with fish, red with meat? _____

Your favourite winemaker or vineyard. _____

The most valuable bottle you own. _____

The most undervalued bottle you own. _____

What wine do you wish you could taste? _____

Your favourite partner in wine. _____

Restaurant you frequent for its wine list. _____

What bottle of wine makes the best hostess gift? _____

Every wine collection should include: _____

Your favourite time to enjoy a glass. _____

Your favourite wine accessory. _____

Your choice aperitif. _____

Your best adviser. _____

Your favourite book on wine. _____

What country would you visit for its vineyards? _____

Your favourite champagne. _____

If you could drink only one wine for the rest of your life, what would it be? _____

Your favourite wine quote or motto. _____

Your first wine memory. _____

Are you Burgundy or Bordeaux? _____

New World or Old World? _____

Your favourite region. _____

The best wine you ever tasted. _____

Your favourite food and wine pairing. _____

What is your favourite exception to this rule: white with fish, red with meat? _____

Your favourite winemaker or vineyard. _____

The most valuable bottle you own. _____

The most undervalued bottle you own. _____

What wine do you wish you could taste? _____

Your favourite partner in wine. _____

Restaurant you frequent for its wine list. _____

What bottle of wine makes the best hostess gift? _____

Every wine collection should include: _____

Your favourite time to enjoy a glass. _____

Your favourite wine accessory. _____

Your choice aperitif. _____

Your best adviser. _____

Your favourite book on wine. _____

What country would you visit for its vineyards? _____

Your favourite champagne. _____

If you could drink only one wine for the rest of your life, what would it be? _____

Your favourite wine quote or motto. _____

Your first wine memory. _____

Are you Burgundy or Bordeaux? _____

New World or Old World? _____

Your favourite region. _____

The best wine you ever tasted. _____

Your favourite food and wine pairing. _____

What is your favourite exception to this rule: white with fish, red with meat? _____

Your favourite winemaker or vineyard. _____

The most valuable bottle you own. _____

The most undervalued bottle you own. _____

What wine do you wish you could taste? _____

Your favourite partner in wine. _____

Restaurant you frequent for its wine list. _____

What bottle of wine makes the best hostess gift? _____

Every wine collection should include: _____

Your favourite time to enjoy a glass. _____

Your favourite wine accessory. _____

Your choice aperitif. _____

Your best adviser. _____

Your favourite book on wine. _____

What country would you visit for its vineyards? _____

Your favourite champagne. _____

If you could drink only one wine for the rest of your life, what would it be? _____

Your favourite wine quote or motto. _____

Your first wine memory. _____

Are you Burgundy or Bordeaux? _____

New World or Old World? _____

Your favourite region. _____

The best wine you ever tasted. _____

Your favourite food and wine pairing. _____

What is your favourite exception to this rule: white with fish, red with meat? _____

Your favourite winemaker or vineyard. _____

The most valuable bottle you own. _____

The most undervalued bottle you own. _____

What wine do you wish you could taste? _____

Your favourite partner in wine. _____

Restaurant you frequent for its wine list. _____

What bottle of wine makes the best hostess gift? _____

Every wine collection should include: _____

Your favourite time to enjoy a glass. _____

Your favourite wine accessory. _____

Your choice aperitif. _____

Your best adviser. _____

Your favourite book on wine. _____

What country would you visit for its vineyards? _____

Your favourite champagne. _____

If you could drink only one wine for the rest of your life, what would it be? _____

Your favourite wine quote or motto. _____

Your first wine memory.

Are you Burgundy or Bordeaux?

New World or Old World?

Your favourite region.

The best wine you ever tasted.

Your favourite food and wine pairing.

What is your favourite exception to this rule: white with fish, red with meat?

Your favourite winemaker or vineyard.

The most valuable bottle you own.

The most undervalued bottle you own.

What wine do you wish you could taste?

Your favourite partner in wine.

Restaurant you frequent for its wine list.

What bottle of wine makes the best hostess gift?

Every wine collection should include:

Your favourite time to enjoy a glass.

Your favourite wine accessory.

Your choice aperitif.

Your best adviser.

Your favourite book on wine.

What country would you visit for its vineyards?

Your favourite champagne.

If you could drink only one wine for the rest of your life, what would it be?

Your favourite wine quote or motto.

Your first wine memory. _____

Are you Burgundy or Bordeaux? _____

New World or Old World? _____

Your favourite region. _____

The best wine you ever tasted. _____

Your favourite food and wine pairing. _____

What is your favourite exception to this rule: white with fish, red with meat? ____

Your favourite winemaker or vineyard. _____

The most valuable bottle you own. _____

The most undervalued bottle you own. _____

What wine do you wish you could taste? _____

Your favourite partner in wine. _____

Restaurant you frequent for its wine list. _____

What bottle of wine makes the best hostess gift? _____

Every wine collection should include: _____

Your favourite time to enjoy a glass. _____

Your favourite wine accessory. _____

Your choice aperitif. _____

Your best adviser. _____

Your favourite book on wine. _____

What country would you visit for its vineyards? _____

Your favourite champagne. _____

If you could drink only one wine for the rest of your life, what would it be? _____

Your favourite wine quote or motto. _____

Your first wine memory. _____

Are you Burgundy or Bordeaux? _____

New World or Old World? _____

Your favourite region. _____

The best wine you ever tasted. _____

Your favourite food and wine pairing. _____

What is your favourite exception to this rule: white with fish, red with meat? ____

Your favourite winemaker or vineyard. _____

The most valuable bottle you own. _____

The most undervalued bottle you own. _____

What wine do you wish you could taste? _____

Your favourite partner in wine. _____

Restaurant you frequent for its wine list. _____

What bottle of wine makes the best hostess gift? _____

Every wine collection should include: _____

Your favourite time to enjoy a glass. _____

Your favourite wine accessory. _____

Your choice aperitif. _____

Your best adviser. _____

Your favourite book on wine. _____

What country would you visit for its vineyards? _____

Your favourite champagne. _____

If you could drink only one wine for the rest of your life, what would it be? _____

Your favourite wine quote or motto. _____

Your first wine memory. _____

Are you Burgundy or Bordeaux? _____

New World or Old World? _____

Your favourite region. _____

The best wine you ever tasted. _____

Your favourite food and wine pairing. _____

What is your favourite exception to this rule: white with fish, red with meat? _____

Your favourite winemaker or vineyard. _____

The most valuable bottle you own. _____

The most undervalued bottle you own. _____

What wine do you wish you could taste? _____

Your favourite partner in wine. _____

Restaurant you frequent for its wine list. _____

What bottle of wine makes the best hostess gift? _____

Every wine collection should include: _____

Your favourite time to enjoy a glass. _____

Your favourite wine accessory. _____

Your choice aperitif. _____

Your best adviser. _____

Your favourite book on wine. _____

What country would you visit for its vineyards? _____

Your favourite champagne. _____

If you could drink only one wine for the rest of your life, what would it be? _____

Your favourite wine quote or motto. _____

Your first wine memory. _____

Are you Burgundy or Bordeaux? _____

New World or Old World? _____

Your favourite region. _____

The best wine you ever tasted. _____

Your favourite food and wine pairing. _____

What is your favourite exception to this rule: white with fish, red with meat? ____

Your favourite winemaker or vineyard. _____

The most valuable bottle you own. _____

The most undervalued bottle you own. _____

What wine do you wish you could taste? _____

Your favourite partner in wine. _____

Restaurant you frequent for its wine list. _____

What bottle of wine makes the best hostess gift? _____

Every wine collection should include: _____

Your favourite time to enjoy a glass. _____

Your favourite wine accessory. _____

Your choice aperitif. _____

Your best adviser. _____

Your favourite book on wine. _____

What country would you visit for its vineyards? _____

Your favourite champagne. _____

If you could drink only one wine for the rest of your life, what would it be? _____

Your favourite wine quote or motto. _____

Your first wine memory. _____

Are you Burgundy or Bordeaux? _____

New World or Old World? _____

Your favourite region. _____

The best wine you ever tasted. _____

Your favourite food and wine pairing. _____

What is your favourite exception to this rule: white with fish, red with meat? _____

Your favourite winemaker or vineyard. _____

The most valuable bottle you own. _____

The most undervalued bottle you own. _____

What wine do you wish you could taste? _____

Your favourite partner in wine. _____

Restaurant you frequent for its wine list. _____

What bottle of wine makes the best hostess gift? _____

Every wine collection should include: _____

Your favourite time to enjoy a glass. _____

Your favourite wine accessory. _____

Your choice aperitif. _____

Your best adviser. _____

Your favourite book on wine. _____

What country would you visit for its vineyards? _____

Your favourite champagne. _____

If you could drink only one wine for the rest of your life, what would it be? _____

Your favourite wine quote or motto. _____

Your first wine memory. _____

Are you Burgundy or Bordeaux? _____

New World or Old World? _____

Your favourite region. _____

The best wine you ever tasted. _____

Your favourite food and wine pairing. _____

What is your favourite exception to this rule: white with fish, red with meat? _____

Your favourite winemaker or vineyard. _____

The most valuable bottle you own. _____

The most undervalued bottle you own. _____

What wine do you wish you could taste? _____

Your favourite partner in wine. _____

Restaurant you frequent for its wine list. _____

What bottle of wine makes the best hostess gift? _____

Every wine collection should include: _____

Your favourite time to enjoy a glass. _____

Your favourite wine accessory. _____

Your choice aperitif. _____

Your best adviser. _____

Your favourite book on wine. _____

What country would you visit for its vineyards? _____

Your favourite champagne. _____

If you could drink only one wine for the rest of your life, what would it be? _____

Your favourite wine quote or motto. _____

Your first wine memory.

Are you Burgundy or Bordeaux?

New World or Old World?

Your favourite region.

The best wine you ever tasted.

Your favourite food and wine pairing.

What is your favourite exception to this rule: white with fish, red with meat?

Your favourite winemaker or vineyard.

The most valuable bottle you own.

The most undervalued bottle you own.

What wine do you wish you could taste?

Your favourite partner in wine.

Restaurant you frequent for its wine list.

What bottle of wine makes the best hostess gift?

Every wine collection should include:

Your favourite time to enjoy a glass.

Your favourite wine accessory.

Your choice aperitif.

Your best adviser.

Your favourite book on wine.

What country would you visit for its vineyards?

Your favourite champagne.

If you could drink only one wine for the rest of your life, what would it be?

Your favourite wine quote or motto.

Your first wine memory. _____

Are you Burgundy or Bordeaux? _____

New World or Old World? _____

Your favourite region. _____

The best wine you ever tasted. _____

Your favourite food and wine pairing. _____

What is your favourite exception to this rule: white with fish, red with meat? _____

Your favourite winemaker or vineyard. _____

The most valuable bottle you own. _____

The most undervalued bottle you own. _____

What wine do you wish you could taste? _____

Your favourite partner in wine. _____

Restaurant you frequent for its wine list. _____

What bottle of wine makes the best hostess gift? _____

Every wine collection should include: _____

Your favourite time to enjoy a glass. _____

Your favourite wine accessory. _____

Your choice aperitif. _____

Your best adviser. _____

Your favourite book on wine. _____

What country would you visit for its vineyards? _____

Your favourite champagne. _____

If you could drink only one wine for the rest of your life, what would it be? _____

Your favourite wine quote or motto. _____

Your first wine memory. _____

Are you Burgundy or Bordeaux? _____

New World or Old World? _____

Your favourite region. _____

The best wine you ever tasted. _____

Your favourite food and wine pairing. _____

What is your favourite exception to this rule: white with fish, red with meat? _____

Your favourite winemaker or vineyard. _____

The most valuable bottle you own. _____

The most undervalued bottle you own. _____

What wine do you wish you could taste? _____

Your favourite partner in wine. _____

Restaurant you frequent for its wine list. _____

What bottle of wine makes the best hostess gift? _____

Every wine collection should include: _____

Your favourite time to enjoy a glass. _____

Your favourite wine accessory. _____

Your choice aperitif. _____

Your best adviser. _____

Your favourite book on wine. _____

What country would you visit for its vineyards? _____

Your favourite champagne. _____

If you could drink only one wine for the rest of your life, what would it be? _____

Your favourite wine quote or motto. _____

Your first wine memory. _____

Are you Burgundy or Bordeaux? _____

New World or Old World? _____

Your favourite region. _____

The best wine you ever tasted. _____

Your favourite food and wine pairing. _____

What is your favourite exception to this rule: white with fish, red with meat? _____

Your favourite winemaker or vineyard. _____

The most valuable bottle you own. _____

The most undervalued bottle you own. _____

What wine do you wish you could taste? _____

Your favourite partner in wine. _____

Restaurant you frequent for its wine list. _____

What bottle of wine makes the best hostess gift? _____

Every wine collection should include: _____

Your favourite time to enjoy a glass. _____

Your favourite wine accessory. _____

Your choice aperitif. _____

Your best adviser. _____

Your favourite book on wine. _____

What country would you visit for its vineyards? _____

Your favourite champagne. _____

If you could drink only one wine for the rest of your life, what would it be? _____

Your favourite wine quote or motto. _____

Your first wine memory. _____

Are you Burgundy or Bordeaux? _____

New World or Old World? _____

Your favourite region. _____

The best wine you ever tasted. _____

Your favourite food and wine pairing. _____

What is your favourite exception to this rule: white with fish, red with meat? _____

Your favourite winemaker or vineyard. _____

The most valuable bottle you own. _____

The most undervalued bottle you own. _____

What wine do you wish you could taste? _____

Your favourite partner in wine. _____

Restaurant you frequent for its wine list. _____

What bottle of wine makes the best hostess gift? _____

Every wine collection should include: _____

Your favourite time to enjoy a glass. _____

Your favourite wine accessory. _____

Your choice aperitif. _____

Your best adviser. _____

Your favourite book on wine. _____

What country would you visit for its vineyards? _____

Your favourite champagne. _____

If you could drink only one wine for the rest of your life, what would it be? _____

Your favourite wine quote or motto. _____

Your first wine memory. _____

Are you Burgundy or Bordeaux? _____

New World or Old World? _____

Your favourite region. _____

The best wine you ever tasted. _____

Your favourite food and wine pairing. _____

What is your favourite exception to this rule: white with fish, red with meat? _____

Your favourite winemaker or vineyard. _____

The most valuable bottle you own. _____

The most undervalued bottle you own. _____

What wine do you wish you could taste? _____

Your favourite partner in wine. _____

Restaurant you frequent for its wine list. _____

What bottle of wine makes the best hostess gift? _____

Every wine collection should include: _____

Your favourite time to enjoy a glass. _____

Your favourite wine accessory. _____

Your choice aperitif. _____

Your best adviser. _____

Your favourite book on wine. _____

What country would you visit for its vineyards? _____

Your favourite champagne. _____

If you could drink only one wine for the rest of your life, what would it be? _____

Your favourite wine quote or motto. _____

Your first wine memory. _____

Are you Burgundy or Bordeaux? _____

New World or Old World? _____

Your favourite region. _____

The best wine you ever tasted. _____

Your favourite food and wine pairing. _____

What is your favourite exception to this rule: white with fish, red with meat? _____

Your favourite winemaker or vineyard. _____

The most valuable bottle you own. _____

The most undervalued bottle you own. _____

What wine do you wish you could taste? _____

Your favourite partner in wine. _____

Restaurant you frequent for its wine list. _____

What bottle of wine makes the best hostess gift? _____

Every wine collection should include: _____

Your favourite time to enjoy a glass. _____

Your favourite wine accessory. _____

Your choice aperitif. _____

Your best adviser. _____

Your favourite book on wine. _____

What country would you visit for its vineyards? _____

Your favourite champagne. _____

If you could drink only one wine for the rest of your life, what would it be? _____

Your favourite wine quote or motto. _____

Your first wine memory.

Are you Burgundy or Bordeaux?

New World or Old World?

Your favourite region.

The best wine you ever tasted.

Your favourite food and wine pairing.

What is your favourite exception to this rule: white with fish, red with meat?

Your favourite winemaker or vineyard.

The most valuable bottle you own.

The most undervalued bottle you own.

What wine do you wish you could taste?

Your favourite partner in wine.

Restaurant you frequent for its wine list.

What bottle of wine makes the best hostess gift?

Every wine collection should include:

Your favourite time to enjoy a glass.

Your favourite wine accessory.

Your choice aperitif.

Your best adviser.

Your favourite book on wine.

What country would you visit for its vineyards?

Your favourite champagne.

If you could drink only one wine for the rest of your life, what would it be?

Your favourite wine quote or motto.

Your first wine memory. _____

Are you Burgundy or Bordeaux? _____

New World or Old World? _____

Your favourite region. _____

The best wine you ever tasted. _____

Your favourite food and wine pairing. _____

What is your favourite exception to this rule: white with fish, red with meat? __

Your favourite winemaker or vineyard. _____

The most valuable bottle you own. _____

The most undervalued bottle you own. _____

What wine do you wish you could taste? _____

Your favourite partner in wine. _____

Restaurant you frequent for its wine list. _____

What bottle of wine makes the best hostess gift? _____

Every wine collection should include: _____

Your favourite time to enjoy a glass. _____

Your favourite wine accessory. _____

Your choice aperitif. _____

Your best adviser. _____

Your favourite book on wine. _____

What country would you visit for its vineyards? _____

Your favourite champagne. _____

If you could drink only one wine for the rest of your life, what would it be? __

Your favourite wine quote or motto. _____

Acknowledgments

The publisher wishes to thank all those who kindly answered the Wine Questionnaire: André Balazs, Mario Batali, Jean-Charles Boisset, Massimo Bottura, Daniel Boulud, Bernard Burtschy, Graydon Carter, Belinda Chang, Sofia Coppola, Martine de la Brosse, Hugo Desnoyer, Michel Dovaz, Lamberto Frescobaldi, Daniel Johnnes, Jay McInerney, Danny Meyer, Robert M. Parker, Jr., Philippe Pascal, Leonid Rath, Joël Robuchon, Benjamin Roffet, and Carolyn Wente.

The Wine Questionnaire   Le Qu

iesling Chardonnay

Vine Questionnaire   The V

on blanc Pinot Noi

merlot   The Wine Questionn

Questionnaire du Vin T

hardonnay   The Wine

Vin   Sauvignon

Le Questionnaire du Vin   The Wi

CHÂTEAU
BORDEAUX
MARGAUX   Le Questionnaire

e Questionnaire du Vin

wine   The Wine Questionnair